Live Justly, edited by Jason Fileta

To purchase copies, visit **www.livejust.ly**,
or for bulk order, contact the publisher:
Micah Challenge USA
1033 SW Yamhill St. Suite #102
Portland, OR 97205

1.888.789.4660 www.micahchallengeusa.org www.livejust.ly

Cover art by Ekko Designs
Cover photograph by Jennifer Wilmore
Interior design: Ekko Designs
Editor: Jason Fileta
Assistant editor: Kimberly Hunt
Contributors: Eugene Cho, Jason Fileta, Kimberly Hunt, Ben Lowe, Lisa Graham McMinn, Shyane Moore, Ronald Sider, Kyle Stillman, Ashley Walker, Nicholas Wolterstorff, and Kimberly McOwen Yim.

Live Justly was created by Micah Challenge USA and developed in conjunction with Bread for the World Institute.

PERMISSIONS

CONTENTS

PART 1 | FOUNDATIONS

PART 2 | LET'S GET PRACTICAL!

PART 3, HOW NOW SHALL WE LIVE?

HELPFUL READING AND TOOLS

WE NEED TO **DO JUSTICE** TO 'DOING JUSTICE'

LIVE JUSTLY

Since 2004, Micah Challenge USA has been mobilizing Christians to end extreme poverty. In that time we have come to believe that, while inspiring action from our supporters, it is unacceptable to use powerful Scriptures like Isaiah 58:6-10, Amos 5, and Luke 4:18 simply to urge advocates to write a letter to congress once a year, volunteer for a day, give to a cause, sign a petition, or share a startling fact on Facebook. **The weight of the call to live justly and the weight of the response need to be balanced.**

Justice is often invoked by passionate teachers, pastors, and leaders inviting us into NEW action. For example, a justice-themed sermon from a leader or pastor often encourages church members to volunteer, go on a mission trip, or give to a cause. Justice is often focused upon doing something new, but what about the actions you and I take every day?

Biblical justice isn't an action once a year, it is a lifestyle.

Here's the thing: **justice isn't always about doing something new; it's about aligning what we already do with Kingdom values.** We wake up every day and make about fifty decisions--we decide what clothes to wear, what food to eat, how to commute to work or school, how to treat our friends, family, and strangers, what to pray for, where to invest our money, and so on. Justice isn't simply an action once a year; it is a lifestyle. Our prayer is that our everyday actions will be infused with justice— not our definition of justice but God's revelation of justice in Scripture.

The Scriptures and the movement of the Holy Spirit have deeply touched our own lives here at Micah Challenge, and the call to seek justice has permeated our everyday life choices—pushing us not just to seek justice but to live justly. Perhaps you too feel that call to seek justice. You are not alone in this experience-- countless churches, campus groups, small groups, families, and individuals have heard the call and asked us, "What's next?"

Enter *Live Justly*.

PRINCIPLES

Live Justly is an in-depth scriptural and practical study to help people live justly in five key areas of life: advocacy, prayer, consumption, generosity, relationships, and creation care. *Live Justly* was written based on these core principles:

> Justice is part of the character and nature of God, and to live justly, we must encounter God in a personal and powerful way.

> The Holy Spirit is the one who convicts.

> People change through relationships, not statistics, so *Live Justly* is designed to create a culture and community among participants that enables honest, convicting discussion about justice.

> We will not reduce justice to simply an activity, it is a lifestyle.

> We will not sacrifice the dignity of people living in oppression for the sake of inspiring action.

> We particularly focus upon the role of advocacy, which is a lost art within the Church, but the ground is fertile for a revival of action that has the potential to be incredibly transformative. We define advocacy as challenging **ourselves** and our **leaders** to change **attitudes**, **behaviors**, and **policies** that perpetuate injustice and deny God's will for all creation to flourish.

HOW TO USE LIVEJUST.LY

This study is designed to help support your community's pursuit of biblical justice in both understanding and practice. *Live Justly* is designed to be used in ten sessions—we recommend doing it over the course of ten or twenty weeks.

Our hope is that, after ten sessions, you will be blessed with the following results:

- Deepened relationships within your small group

- A thorough understanding of and commitment to biblical justice

- Renewed passion and inspiration to live justly

- An individual action plan that shows what practical steps you will take to live justly

- A collective action plan for your group to mobilize your church for justice

Each session includes the following components:

- **A video** to help get everyone on the same page ... just in case you didn't get a chance to read the essay. All the videos are located at **www.livejust.ly**

- **Definitions** to give you the same language to engage with the session's topic

- **A story** to help you see the session's topic played out in real life

- **An essay** to summarize the week's topic concisely, a great source for your group discussion

- **A Scripture passage** to examine how Scripture addresses the session's topic

- **Questions** to help you generate a lively discussion

- **"Together,"** activities for you to do as a group to help cement the concepts

- **Solo work** to help you process the small-group time, reflect, pray, and slowly develop a personal action plan

- **Key resources** located at **www.livejust.ly** to dig deeper into issues raised in the session, which can be assigned as homework

A WORD ABOUT THE LOGO

The *Live Justly* logo is a visual representation of our hopes and dreams for this curriculum:

Each side of the hexagon represents one facet of life you will be inspired to live justly in: advocacy, prayer, consumption, generosity, creation care, and relationships.

The circle represents the holistic nature of living justly. If we are incredible advocates but do so at the expense of our personal relationships, then the circle is broken. If we are compassionate to the impoverished but fail to challenge unjust structures that cause their oppression, then too, the circle is broken. The circle represents a holistic, unified lifestyle of justice.

The fire symbolizes our posture of worship. We live justly not as the Pharisees did, seeking to follow the law as a checklist, but rather recognizing that justice is part of the character of God and living justly in response to God.

The bread symbolizes the essential need for community. We cannot live justly without pursuing authentic community. The circle will break if it is not held together by many hands and voices.

LET'S DO THIS

This curriculum will not give you a prescription for living justly, but our prayer is that you will encounter God, be influenced by the Holy Spirit, sharpen your passions, and find community that spurs you to renewed action. We are excited and honored to journey with you to live justly!

WHAT IS BIBLICAL JUSTICE?

A THEOLOGY OF JUSTICE

If you are trying to live a life in accordance with the Bible, the concept and call to justice are inescapable.

-Tim Keller

It's not just about doing justice, this journey is also about allowing the work of justice to change us. In other words, we not only seek justice as we follow Jesus, but we seek to live justly. Our calling is not simply to change the world but perhaps as important, our calling is to be changed ourselves.

-Eugene Cho

DEFINITIONS

BIBLICAL JUSTICE

The state of wholeness due all of God's creation.
Justice is required for Shalom.

SHALOM

Hebrew word for peace, completeness, and wholeness.
Where there is justice, there will be shalom.

PRIMARY JUSTICE

One type of justice found in Scripture referring to the
rights due all of creation by mere fact of being created by God.

REACTIVE JUSTICE

Another type of Justice in Scripture, defined as giving what is
due in response to a violation of primary justice; most often used
in reference to the judicial system.

YEAR OF JUBILEE

Every 50 years, the Israelites were to partake in a year of
celebration and liberation. They would restore lands, property,
and property rights to original owners, and slaves would be sent
home to their families (Leviticus 25).

THE LIMITS OF "JUSTICE"

BY KIM HUNT

A remote town in Burkina Faso struggles to address the most basic needs of the community. There is little water available to grow crops to feed the people. The nearest health clinic is more than 50 miles away, and a doctor visits only sporadically. There is no school in town, and the closest one is too far away for students to travel there. The local church tries to provide basic education for the children, but their efforts are restricted because the church's capacity is too limited to serve as a fully functional educational facility.

A community church in the United States connects with the local church in Burkina Faso because they are part of the same denomination. They pull together a team of 15 passionate and able people to organize a justice trip—recently rebranded from a "short- term mission" trip. They raise thousands of dollars, fly thousands of miles, and arrive to help. They work tirelessly alongside the Burkina community, building a school. For 10 days, they engage in fellowship, pray, and work alongside one another building what will be the community's first school. The American team leaves with heavy hearts, knowing that their new friends will continue to struggle, but also hopeful that the opportunity for education will open doors for the future generation.

They pray more, they give more to missions, but some wonder why justice feels so incomplete.

The Burkina community resumes life. The community has a beautiful new school building for the children near the center of town. However, there is no teacher to teach at the school, no food in the children's stomachs to help them concentrate, and many of them are sick because the water they're drinking is unsafe and there are no doctors around to help treat them.

Thousands of miles away, the church in the U.S. shares photos and stories from their justice trip. As time passes, they struggle to figure out how to live justly and support their friends in Burkina Faso. They pray more, they give more to missions, but some wonder why justice feels so incomplete. Perhaps, they wonder, it wasn't a "justice" trip after all.

GOD LOVES JUSTICE

BY NICHOLAS WOLTERSTORFF

There is a clear way of thinking about justice in the Scriptures—and what those writings say about justice is an inextricable component of the message. **Pull out justice, and everything unravels.**

Some of the skeptics of justice in Scripture are secularists who have gotten the impression that Christianity is all about love and not about justice. A good many of the skeptics are Christians who are committed to interpreting Scripture solely through the lens of love. And then there are those who concede that Scripture speaks of justice but assume that it refers to Kings and courts in the administration of justice. When I say that justice is an inextricable component of the biblical message, I have in mind primary justice.

PRIMARY & REACTIVE

There are two different kinds of justice in Scripture: primary justice and reactive justice.

Reactive justice punishes the wrongdoer, condemns the wrongdoer, is perhaps angry with the wrongdoer, and so forth—reacting to one's wrongdoing. Reactive justice renders justice to a wrongdoer.

What that implies, obviously, is that reactive justice is relevant when there someone has treated another person unjustly. And what that implies, in turn, is that **reactive justice cannot be the only kind of justice.** There has to be another kind of justice, a kind of justice such that, when someone violates this other kind of justice and is thus a wrongdoer, reactive justice becomes relevant.

I am going to call it **primary justice.**

Reactive justice becomes relevant when there has been a violation of primary justice.

God loves justice. God has a heart for justice. God is devoted to justice. So it comes as no surprise that God says to: "Seek justice; do justice; let justice roll down like waters; imitate me in loving justice." But is God speaking of reactive justice, reserved for courts, kings, and judges, or primary justice, which applies to all people? I believe that, in many cases, these Scriptures are speaking of primary justice.

MISHPAT & TSEDEQA

The Hebrew word in the Old Testament that is usually translated into English as "justice" is "misphat." The term is often paired with "tsedeqa," typically translated as "righteousness." Together, they are often translated as "justice and righteousness" in the Old Testament and simply "righteousness" in the New Testament. My own sense is that, when the rhetorical context permits, "tsedeqa" is better rendered into present-day English as the right thing, going right, or doing right. The word "righteous" is almost never used anymore in ordinary speech, and when it is, it suggests a person intensely preoccupied with his own moral character who has few sins to his debit. The connotation is self-righteousness. **The pairing of "misphat" and "tsedeqa" is better translated as "primary justice" or simply "justice" than as "justice and righteousness" or simply "righteousness."**

Such a reading of Scripture would require us to read Amos 5:24 and Micah 6:8 as applying to all people, not simply kings and judges. Additionally, this reading of Scripture would mean that Jesus blessed those who "hunger and thirst for justice." Once again, pull out justice, and everything unravels.

God loves the pair "mishpat" and "tsedeqa," primary justice. But why?

Scripture teaches that what God wants for God's human family is what the OT writers called, in Hebrew, shalom. "Shalom" is almost always translated as "peace" in our English Bibles. I think that is a very poor translation. Shalom is much more than peace. Shalom is flourishing. What God desires for us is that we flourish in all dimensions of our existence.

> *In the absence of justice, we are not truly flourishing; in the absence of justice, shalom is impaired.*

And now for the point relevant to our purposes here: when you read what the biblical writers say about shalom, it soon becomes clear that shalom requires justice. **In the absence of justice, we are not truly flourishing; in the absence of justice, shalom is impaired.** Shalom goes beyond justice but always includes It. Justice is, you might say, the ground floor of shalom. So once again, why does God love justice? Because God loves shalom, and shalom includes justice.

When the kingdom of God has come in its fullness, there will be no breaches of primary justice and hence no reactive justice; all justice will be primary justice. **You and I are to image God by also having a heart for justice.**

ISAIAH 61

QUESTIONS FOR DISCUSSION

1. What is God's definition of justice?
2. Why do you think Jesus quoted this passage from Isaiah in his first Sermon in Luke 4:18?
3. In the absence of the Year of Jubilee, how do we ensure a "reset" to undo the structural and personal sin that perpetuates injustice?
4. What is God saying to you, and what are you going to do about it?

TOGETHER

How have you defined "justice" in the past? As a small group, create a practical and biblical definition of justice. Use the essay above, your own experiences and ideas, and Scripture. You'll use this definition for the rest of your time journeying together.

SOLO WORK

Read Luke 4:16-21. With a knowledge of Jesus' work displayed in the Gospels and the context of God's desire for justice detailed in Isaiah 61, explain Jesus' words, "The Scripture you've just heard has been fulfilled this very day!"

- How does Jesus' work on earth fulfill Isaiah 61?

- How is this session's message and discussion challenging you? Are you one who knows God but has resisted justice? Are you much more comfortable with justice but have resisted God?

Journal about this. Be vulnerable. Be open.
This is between you and God.

PRAYER

Lord, you know my heart. If I have claimed to know you but have resisted seeking justice, forgive me. If I have passionately sought justice but been detached from you, draw me near to you. Help me recognize your Spirit in me and respond to your call to seek justice.

SESSION TWO
INTEGRAL MISSION
JUSTICE AND OUR MISSION IN THE WORLD

If we ignore the world we betray the word of God which sends us out to serve the world. If we ignore the word of God we have nothing to bring to the world
-Micah Declaration on Integral Mission

The risen Jesus expects that his disciple-community which is preaching the Good News among the nations is also striving at Christian unity, is sharing its resources with the poor and needy, is engaged in costly initiatives of peacemaking, and hungering and thirsting after God's justice
-Vinoth Ramachandra

DEFINITIONS

INTEGRAL MISSION

The proclamation and demonstration of the gospel. It is not simply that evangelism and social involvement are to be done alongside each other; rather, it is in integral mission that our proclamation has social consequences as we call people to love and repentance in all areas of life, and our social involvement has evangelistic consequences as we bear witness to the transforming grace of Jesus Christ.[1]

CHURCH

The body of disciples established by Jesus for the advancement of the kingdom of God on earth through preaching the good news and making disciples.

KINGDOM OF GOD

The place where God's justice reigns and shalom is achieved. All things are made right. The Kingdom is already here, but not in fullness. We will only see glimpses of the Kingdom until Christ's return.

---

1 Read the Micah Declaration on Integral Mission in its entirety on pp. 111-116

DISCONNECTED MISSIONS VS. INTEGRAL MISSIONS

BY JASON FILETA

When I was 14, I went on a mission trip to inner-city Chicago. I should stress this wasn't an "integral" mission trip but a "disconnected" mission trip. We went to preach the Gospel to a hurting community. Now, there were a number of missteps along the way— we assumed they didn't have the Gospel, we assumed the Spirit wasn't alive there already, and we assumed that preaching the Gospel simply meant winning souls through convincing or shaming people enough to say "the prayer." So, how did it go?

I remember being proud of how God used me. There was a homeless man whose breath smelled of alcohol whom I successfully brought to tears over the guilt of his mistakes and then restored through passionate prayer on our knees on the sidewalk a block away from Cabrini Green.

IN ALL OF THE GOOD I REMEMBER DOING, I ALSO REMEMBER FEELING LIKE SOMETHING WAS MISSING.

Yet despite all the good I remember doing, I also remember feeling as if something was missing. Sure, he prayed the prayer, but was he sincere? Was he even sober? When Jesus forgave sins, he often physically healed the body—he brought integral wholeness to individuals, families, and sometimes communities. Could I pull this off in sixty minutes on a street corner? I had convinced a drunk man to repeat after me, without offering any wholeness to the brokenness of his body— his hunger, his lack of affordable housing, his alcoholism, etc.

He was going to wake up the next day in the same broken place as the day we prayed—wasn't there more to it? I was only 14, but I knew something was missing.

Unfortunately, it wasn't until I read the Bible nearly five years later that I realized that, by proclaiming the good news without demonstration (in which authentic relationship is required), I'm not really preaching the good news of Jesus Christ. I'm preaching a modified version that has the aroma of the good news but isn't THE good news.

"INTEGRAL MISSION"
BY RENE PADILLA

Although it has recently become fashionable to use the term "integral mission," the approach to mission that it expresses is not new. The practice of integral mission goes back to Jesus himself and to the first-century Christian church. Furthermore, a growing number of churches are putting this style of mission into practice without necessarily using this expression to refer to what they are doing: integral mission is not part of their vocabulary. It is clear that the practice of integral mission is much more important than the use of this new expression to refer to it.

The expression "integral mission" (misión integral) came into use principally within the Latin American Theological Fraternity (FTL) about twenty years ago. It was an attempt to highlight the importance of conceiving the mission of the church within a more biblical theological framework than the traditional one, which had been accepted in evangelical circles due to the influence of the modern missionary movement. What is this approach to mission? In what respects does it differ from the traditional transcultural approach?

[VIEW CHART PAGES 26-27]

INTEGRAL MISSION, A NEW PARADIGM
From the perspective of integral mission, traditional transcultural mission is far from exhausting the significance of the mission of the church. Mission may or may not include a crossing of geographical frontiers, but in every case, it means primarily a crossing of the frontier between faith and no faith, whether in one's own country (at home) or in a foreign country (on the mission field), according to the testimony to Jesus Christ as Lord of the whole of life and of the whole of creation.

When the church is committed to integral mission and to communicating the gospel through everything it is, does, and says, it understands that its goal is not to become large numerically, nor to be rich materially, nor powerful politically. Its purpose is to incarnate the values of the Kingdom of God and witness to the love and the justice revealed in Jesus Christ, by the power of the Spirit, for the transformation of human life in all its dimensions, both on the individual level and on the community level.

The accomplishment of this purpose presupposes that all the members of the church, without exception, by the very fact of having become a part of the Body of Christ, receive gifts and ministries for the exercise of their priesthood, to which they have been ordained in their baptism. Mission is not the responsibility and privilege of a small group of the faithful who feel called to the mission field (usually in a foreign country) but of all members since all are members of the royal priesthood and as such have been called by God to declare the praises of him who called them out of darkness into his wonderful light (1 Pet 2.9) wherever they may be.

Understood in these terms, this new paradigm for mission is not so new; it is, rather, the recovery of the biblical concept of mission since, in effect, mission is faithful to the teaching of Scripture to the extent that it is placed at the service of the Kingdom of God and God's justice.

Integral mission is the means designed by God to carry out, throughout history, his purpose of love and justice revealed in Jesus Christ through the Church and in the power of the Spirit.

INTEGRAL MISSION

1. All churches send and all churches receive. The road of mission is not a one-way street. It does not go only from Christian countries to the pagan countries; it is a two-way street.

2. The whole world is a mission field, and every human need is an opportunity for missionary service. The local church is called to demonstrate the reality of the Kingdom of God among the kingdoms of this world, not only by what it says but also by what it is and by what it does in response to human needs on every side.

3. Every Christian is called to follow Jesus Christ and to be committed to God's mission in the world. The benefits of salvation are inseparable from a missionary lifestyle, and this implies, among other things, the practice of the universal priesthood of believers in all spheres of human life according to the gifts and ministries that the Spirit of God has freely bestowed on his people.

4. The Christian life on both the individual and the community levels, is the primary witness to the universal lordship of Jesus Christ and the transforming power of the Holy Spirit. Mission is much more than words; it is demonstrated in the life that recovers God's original purpose for the relationship of the human person with the Creator, with neighbor, and with all of creation.

TRADITIONAL TRANSCULTURAL MISSION

1. Some churches send, almost exclusively from Western Christianity, and some churches receive, almost exclusively from the Global South.

---

2. Only the receiving country is viewed as a mission field. The missionaries "home" is usually somewhere in the Christian West, and their "mission field" is located in some pagan country. It is not surprising that a majority of career missionaries decide to retire in their home country.

---

3. Only some Christians are missionaries. There are missionaries, called by God to serve him, and then there are common ordinary Christians, who enjoy the benefits of salvation but are exempt from sharing in what God wants to do in the world.

---

4. The life of the church and the mission of the church can be separated. If for a church to be a missionary church, it were sufficient to send and support a few of its members to serve in foreign missions, it is possible that such a church had no significant influence or impact on its surrounding neighborhood. The life of the church is local (at home), and mission takes place in another setting, preferably in a foreign country (the mission field).

MATTHEW 22:34-40 & 28:16

QUESTIONS

1. According to integral mission, any work of the church to usher in the Kingdom of God is mission—do you agree with this? What activities become "missions" that have not typically been identified as such?
2. Can we fulfill the great commission without seeking justice? Why or why not?
3. Has preaching/teaching on the great commission ever compelled you to pursue justice?
4. What is God saying to you, and what are you going to do about it?

TOGETHER

On a piece of paper, make two columns with the headings "Integral Mission" and "Disconnected Mission." Have each person describe his or her own mission experiences—short-term mission trips, mission weeks, etc.—and write the experience and his or her name in the column their mission work falls under.

What are your observations?

Discuss the activities that fall under the "disconnected missions" list and come up with ways you could reshape that activity to be more integral.

SOLO WORK

Begin to work on a creative expression[2] of your understanding
of justice and any story, issue, or Scripture that affects your
understanding of justice. You will continue to work on this
creative expression each session and share with one another in
session 10 (if you feel comfortable).

Submit your creative expression online, and we will build an
archive of Inspiration! Creative expressions include poetry,
spoken word, visual art (painting, drawing, or photography),
short stories, music, and anything else that makes your right
brain come alive!

PRAYER CHALLENGE

*Lord, make me an instrument of your Kingdom. Help me to be
missional even when it is uncomfortable—help me to challenge
the economic, political, and social systems of our world that are in
need of redemption. Help me to proclaim bravely the good news
to my neighbors near and far, and may many come to know and
follow you.*

---

2 Visit www.livejust.ly/creative for samples & ideas to inspire your creativity

JUSTICE, CHARITY, AND ADVOCACY

ADVOCACY AND CHARITY UNITE!

We give people fish. We teach them to fish. We tear down the walls that have been built up around the fish pond. And we figure out who polluted it. **-Shane Claiborne**

We won't end hunger by securing more food, but by securing more justice **-Anonymous**

DEFINITIONS

RELIEF

Assistance, generally one-time or short-term, in the form of food, clothing, or money offered to a person or group of people in crisis.

CHARITY

A voluntary act or gift contributed to those in need, given out of compassion or love.

BIBLICAL JUSTICE

The state of wholeness and flourishing due all of God's creation.

STRUCTURAL INJUSTICE

Sin that infects the systems that govern society such as economic and public policy.

"AMBULANCE DRIVERS OR TUNNEL BUILDERS" °

BY RON SIDER

A group of devout Christians once lived in a small village at the foot of a mountain. A winding, slippery road with hairpin curves and steep precipices without guardrails wound its way up one side of the mountain and down the other. There were frequent fatal accidents. Deeply saddened by the injured people who were pulled from the wrecked cars, the Christians in the village's three churches decided to act. They pooled their resources and purchased an ambulance. Over the years, they saved many lives, although some victims remained crippled for life.

Then one day a visitor came to town. Puzzled, he asked why they did not close the road over the mountain and build a tunnel instead. Startled at first, the ambulance volunteers quickly pointed out that this approach (although technically quite possible) was not realistic or advisable. After all, the narrow mountain road had been there for a long time. Besides, the mayor of the town would bitterly oppose the idea. (He owned a large restaurant and service station halfway up the mountain.)

The visitor was shocked that the mayor's economic interests mattered more to these Christians than the many human casualties. Somewhat hesitantly, he suggested that perhaps the churches ought to speak to the mayor. Perhaps they should even elect a different mayor if he proved stubborn and unconcerned. Now the Christians were shocked. With rising indignation and righteous conviction, they informed the young radical that the church dare not become involved in politics. The church is called to preach the gospel and give a cup of cold water, they said. Its mission is not to dabble in worldly things like social and political structures.

Perplexed and bitter, the visitor left. As he wandered out of the village, one question churned round and round in his muddled mind. Is it really more spiritual, he wondered, to operate the ambulances that pick up the bloody victims of destructive social structures than to try to change the social structures themselves?

"THE CIRCLE OF JUSTICE"
BY JASON FILETA

A few years ago, I spoke at a conference to inspire support for a bill we were working on at Micah Challenge called the Jubilee Act. Essentially, 67 nations were servicing debts to our government at the expense of the ability to provide healthcare, education, and water to their people. The debts they were repaying, some of them decades old, were often lent irresponsibly to dictators at very high interest rates, and we were punishing the citizens of these nations by requiring the repayment of this debt. It was a justice issue.

It was a justice issue that could only be resolved with effective and prophetic advocacy. We could try to set up hospitals, schools, and feeding programs in those 67 nations, but the underlying cause of their inability to do it themselves would still exist: their debt. My role was to inspire the attendees of this conference not just to look upon the hungry with compassion and give them bread but also to cause them to ask why they were hungry—to take decisive action to fix an unjust policy.

After the conference was over, the other speakers and I went out for dinner. At dinner, I mentioned some of the things I had been struggling with at the conference and many other justice and advocacy conferences I had spoken at previously. I was bothered by the disconnectedness of our principles of justice and how we actually ran the conference. The voices of impoverished were often absent, food and other resources were often wasted, and the opportunities for generosity and charitable acts were few or none. The opportunities for advocacy were many, but advocacy alone seemed incomplete.

One of the other speakers essentially told me that I needed to relax and remember why I do what I do. She explained that she lived in a huge house, in a comfortable, safe neighborhood, and indulged in a nice glass of wine and fine food because that was what she deserved, or it what was needed to keep her going in the fight for justice. She implied that she (or I, for that matter) didn't need to be radically generous or consume less for the sake of giving more directly to the impoverished because she was dealing with the structural causes of injustice. We didn't need to be bothered with small acts of charity.

Something didn't feel right.

Here is the reality. Advocacy is not justice. Charity is not justice. The picture of justice we see in Scripture is a prerequisite for shalom—a time when all brokenness is made right. When relationships between people are healed, relationships between people and God are healed, relationships between people and systems are healed, relationships between people and creation are healed, and one's own relationship with oneself is healed.

Advocacy and charity are certainly essential components of justice and therefore shalom, but neither is a synonym for justice. For so long, we've seen people hungry—no matter how much we feed them. This has led to a movement to work for an end to hunger not by delivering more food but by delivering more justice through advocating to governments and corporations for more just policies and practices. Let me tell you something—it is fun to be an advocate. Sometimes, it is exhilarating. To know that your work helped create a level playing field is incredible. To stand in the halls of power and speak prophetically is euphoric (and scary!). I imagine it is similar (although on a much smaller scale) to the exhilaration Moses felt leading the Israelites out of slavery in Egypt.

In fact, a lot of advocates (myself included) use the story of Moses and the Exodus to highlight the essential role of advocacy. God called Moses to go to Pharaoh, the political leader of the day, and release the Israelites from slavery. He didn't call Moses to go the Israelites and comfort, feed, and clothe them through setting up a charity while not addressing the cause of their suffering. But does this mean that God was not concerned about their immediate needs being met? Returning to the issue of hunger in our day, does this mean that God is not concerned about the hungry being fed while we dismantle unjust policies that cause hunger?

ABSOLUTELY NOT!

The whole of Scripture points to a God who wants to see the "captives released, the hungry fed, and naked clothed." Advocacy alone will not accomplish this. Neither will charity alone.

I am certain that, though Moses' calling as an advocate was unique, there were others, perhaps thousands, called to radical acts of charity and generosity to clothe, comfort, and feed the Israelites while still in slavery. It is only consistent with our God that he called compassionate people to be His presence among the Israelites. **Both callings were necessary, both are worthy, and both are part of the call to do justice.**

Advocacy and charity are certainly essential components of justice and therefore shalom, but neither is a synonym for justice.

Biblical justice is holistic in nature. It is a circle made up of many points. If we are tireless advocates but it comes at the expense of our personal relationships, then the circle is broken. If we are compassionate to the impoverished through charity and generosity but fail to challenge the unjust structures that cause their oppression, then, too, the circle is broken.

To see justice truly done, we must become competent and committed to a holistic lifestyle of justice that includes charity and advocacy. We must not choose one over the other but rather recognize what our unique calling is while still embracing the other things that God calls us to in a lifestyle of justice. **Let the circle be unbroken!**

EXODUS 3

QUESTIONS

1. If Moses were called to release those in slavery today, what do you think the church would think of his strategy?
2. Can you think of an example of good-intentioned Christians trying to combat injustice through charity alone? Did it free people?
3. Consider the issue of hunger—what are ways in which you can respond to the hungry not just through providing food but also by loosening the chains of injustice?
4. What is God saying to you, and what are you going to do about it?

TOGETHER

As a group, choose one specific justice issue (hunger, trafficking, HIV/AIDS, etc.). Brainstorm what engagement would look like if charity and advocacy united for justice.

Now consider your own engagement with a justice issue you are passionate about. Share which path you tend to gravitate toward: a response of charity, advocacy, or a mixture of both?

How are you feeling challenged to engage the issue you are passionate about in a new way?

SOLO WORK

Consider a justice issue facing your community. Identify the problem, and search for the root cause by continuing to ask, "Why?"
Now consider the existing responses to the problem. Are they treating the symptoms, the root, or both?

Continue work on your creative expression.

PRAYER

Lord, give me eyes to see the structures and systems that perpetuate injustice. Help me to not have such big eyes that I don't see the immediate needs of the oppressed, and may I never seek justice at the expense of being charitable. Give me a courageous voice to hold my leaders accountable to how their decisions affect the vulnerable.

SESSION FOUR
JUSTICE AND ADVOCACY

TRANSFORMATIONAL ADVOCACY AND THE ROLE OF GOVERNMENT IN SECURING JUSTICE

Doing justice will include changing your lifestyle and habits, but also includes battling economic, social, and various other systems that perpetuate social injustice leaving the most vulnerable in its wake. We need to fight sinful systems and laws, not just inner demons and personal sin **-Grant Walsh**

It is impossible to ignore the political implications of biblical justice **-Joel Edwards**

I've never been involved in partisan politics—and don't intend to do so now—but global poverty is an issue that rises far above mere politics. It is a moral issue. A compassion issue. And because Jesus commanded us to help the poor, it is an obedience issue! He told us to do all we can to alleviate the pain of our brothers and sisters. **-Rick Warren**

DEFINITIONS

ODIOUS DEBT

A debt accrued by a nation against the interests of the population and used in ways that can be harmful or oppressive to the citizens.

ILLEGITIMATE DEBT

(encompasses odious debt, but goes further):
Irresponsibly incurred debt where the debtor potentially used funds to violate human rights and democratic principles and to exploit the vulnerable. The financial burden is compounded by the overwhelming interest rates, creating an inability to ever conceivably repay the debt. A significant proportion of the population lives without basic human needs being met while the government strives to pay off debt.

G8

(Group of 8): A forum for the governments of the leading eight industrialized nations of the world to come together to discuss issues of global concern. The member states include Canada, France, Germany, Italy, Japan, Russia, the United Kingdom, and the United States.

TRANSFORMATIONAL ADVOCACY

Challenging ourselves and our leaders to change attitudes, behaviors, and policies that perpetuate injustice and deny God's will for all creation to flourish.

PRIVILEGE

An advantage or benefit available to some people and not to others within a society.

"ADVOCACY WORKS!"[3]
BY ASHLEY WALKER

Elinta Kasanga lives in Nguluka Village, Zambia. Elinta remembers a time in her village's history when there was a lack of basic necessities. People couldn't afford health clinic fees or school fees. Most villagers survived on one meal a day and water from local contaminated streams. The lack of basic necessities was due in part to the fact that the government of Zambia owed billions of dollars to other governments all over the world. Money spent servicing debt payments was money not going to help the impoverished.

Christians in the global south called on Christians in the global north to take action, believing it unreasonable to enforce debt payments at the expense of basic necessities of life. Thus, the Jubilee 2000 campaign began, advocating for the cancellation of odious and illegitimate debts that impoverished nations were paying back to nations in the global north. The Year of Jubilee (Leviticus 25) was built upon the assumption that, left unchecked, the social, political, and economic order would wreak havoc upon communities because of greed and unjust practices. Jubilee was a chance to hit the reset button.

3 This story is adapted from the Tearfund UK Video *Campaigning Works*

Jubilee 2000 succeeded and debts were cancelled for qualifying countries, but it didn't stop there. People around the world have continued to campaign, and since 1996, a total of $95 billion of debt has been cancelled.

Now in Elinta's village, there are hospitals fully stocked with medicine. There are no school fees for grades 1–7. The country now has money to invest in water wells, and for the first time, Elinta and her village family can have clean water.

Beyond Nguluka Village, after debts were cancelled,[4]

- 1.5 million children returned to school in Tanzania after the government eliminated school fees.

- 500,000 children in Mozambique received vaccinations.

- Free health care was provided for millions living in rural areas in Zambia, many of whom had never had access to any form of health care before.

- 2,500 new primary schools were created and 28,000 extra teachers were trained, resulting in 98% of Tanzanian children being able to enroll in primary education.

Desmond Tutu once said, "There comes a point where we need to stop just pulling people out of the river. We need to go upstream and find out why they're falling in." Jubilee did just that, and it continues to affect lives over a decade later.

---

4 Statistics from Jubilee USA, One and Oxfam

SOCIAL SIN
BY RON SIDER

It is possible to make oppression legal. Legislators devise unjust laws, and bureaucrats implement the injustice. But God shouts divine woe against rulers who use their official position to write unjust laws and unfair legal decisions. Legalized oppression is an abomination to our God. Therefore, God calls his people to oppose political structures that perpetuate injustice.

There is a long tradition of God's people challenging the political structures of the day, from Moses going to Pharaoh and Esther going to the Persian King, with William Wilberforce seeking to end the transatlantic slave trade, and with Dr. King and the U.S. civil rights movement, all the way up to Christians of today speaking out against corruption and policies that perpetuate injustice.

However, neglect of the biblical teaching on structural injustice or institutionalized evil is one of the most deadly omissions in many parts of the church today. Christians frequently restrict ethics to a narrow class of "personal" sins such as drug abuse and sexual misconduct but ignore the sins of institutionalized racism and unjust economic structures that destroy just as many people.

There is an important difference between consciously willed, individual acts (such as lying to a friend or committing an act of adultery) and participation in evil social structures. Slavery is an example of the latter. So is the Victorian factory system that had ten-year-old children working twelve to sixteen hours a day. Both slavery and child labor were legal, but they destroyed millions of people. They were institutionalized, or structural, evils.

God hates evil economic structures and unjust legal systems because they destroy people by the hundreds and thousands and millions. We can be sure that the just Lord of the universe will destroy wicked rulers and unjust social institutions (see I Kings 21).

Another side of institutionalized evil makes it especially pernicious. Structural evil is so subtle that we become ensnared without fully realizing it. God inspired the prophet Amos to utter some of the harshest words in Scripture against the cultured upper-class women of his day: "hear this word you cows of Bashan ... who oppress the poor, who crush the needy, who say to your husbands, 'bring, that we may drink!' The Lord God has sworn by his holiness that, behold the days are coming when they shall take you away with hooks, even the last of you with fishhooks" (4:1-2).

The women involved may have had a little direct contact with the impoverished peasants. They may never have fully realized that their gorgeous clothes and spirited parties were possible partly because of the sweat and tears of the impoverished. In fact, they may have even been kind on occasion to individuals under oppression. But God called these privileged women "cows" because they participated in a structural evil— **lives sustained by the oppression of others. Before God, they were personally and individually guilty.**

If we are members of a privileged group that profits from structural evil or whose lives are sustained by the oppression of others, and if we have at least some understanding of the evil yet fail to do what God wants us to do to change things, we stand guilty before God.

Unfair systems and oppressive structures are an abomination to God, and "social sin" is the correct phrase to categorize them. Furthermore, as we understand their evil, we have a moral obligation to do all that God wants us to do to change them. If we do not, we sin. That is the clear implication of Amos' harsh attack on the wealthy women of his day. It is also the clear implication of James 4:17, *"Whoever knows what is right to do and fails to do it, for him it is sin."*

In the New Testament, the word "cosmos" ("world") often conveys the idea of structural evil. In Greek thought, the word "cosmos" referred to the structures of civilized life, especially the patterns of the Greek city-state that were viewed as essentially good. But the biblical writers knew that sin had invaded and distorted the structures and values of society.

Frequently, therefore, the New Testament uses the word "cosmos" to refer, in C. H. Dodd's words, "to human society in so far as it is organized on wrong principles." "When Paul spoke of 'the world' in a moral sense, he was thinking of the totality of people, social systems, values, and traditions in terms of its opposition to God and his redemptive purposes."[5]

> "Whoever knows what is right to do and fails to do it, for him it is sin." James 4:17

Pope John Paul II rightly insisted that evil social structures are "rooted in personal sin." Social evil results from our rebellion against God and our consequent selfishness toward our neighbors. But the accumulation and concentration of many personal sins create structures of sin that are both oppressive and difficult to remove. We will not see transformed systems simply by converting every CEO, every employee of multinational corporations, and every member of Congress. **We will see transformation by preaching the Gospel while dismantling unjust structures and systems through effective advocacy, passionate prayer, and living justly.**

5 Clinton E. Arnold, *Powers of Darkness,* Intervarsity 1992, p. 203

BOOK OF ESTHER
QUESTIONS

1. Why is Esther hesitant to speak to the king at first?
2. What is the value of Mordecai influencing Esther to advocate for her people, and what are the implications for our understanding of political advocacy today?
3. Both Esther's advocacy and the Jubilee 2000 movement were inspired by the call of those in oppression for advocacy to challenge injustice—can you think of examples of this in modern advocacy movements? What is the risk if the oppressed have no voice in our advocacy?
4. Do you believe you are privileged? What is one way to use your privilege to seek justice?
5. Both Esther and Jubilee 2000 show us that engaging government is inevitable when challenging injustice, but do you see a role for government in promoting flourishing?
6. What is God saying to you, and what are you going to do about it?

TOGETHER

Watch the video "Poverty Isn't Over...Yet"[6] as a group and study the impact of poverty- focused development assistance.[7] We'll use this critical and timeless issue as your pilot issue for advocacy action!

Demystify advocacy by pulling out a cell phone and calling your member of Congress on the spot. They're probably not in the office, but that's okay. Put it on speakerphone and have one person leave a message. Whether someone answers the phone or you leave a message, begin by letting your member of Congress know that you are participating in a small group study on justice and presently addressing the importance of advocacy.[8]

Describe how you're learning about the incredible impact (for such a low cost!) of poverty-focused development assistance, and urge your representative to be a champion for the impoverished by protecting this funding in budget negotiations. If you leave a message, invite the representative to respond by calling back a designated member of your group.

---

6 Video is at livejust.ly/four

7 Fact sheet on PFDA on pp. 117-119

8 Call script and instructions on p. 120

SOLO WORK

We advocate to government for two reasons: to stop unjust policies and to encourage just ones. Research and take action on one of each!

- Considering the role of government to promote flourishing, research the effect of foreign assistance and write a personal letter to your member of Congress to protect lifesaving programs that help the impoverished. Use a personal story— why do you care about people in poverty around the world?[9]

- Regarding the stopping of unjust policies, consider writing your member of Congress on the issue of corruption and how it perpetuates extreme poverty. Once again, use a personal story about why you care about ending corruption and how it perpetuates extreme poverty.[10]

- **Begin writing your long-term action plan!** From this session moving forward, you will continue to add to your personal action plan. All of your action commitments should be measureable and time-bound. You'll eventually share this action plan with your group and with us to help remind you of your commitments.

- Action plan, advocacy: What is one way you can speak out and be a voice for justice to our leaders? Commit to something specific— maybe it's a phone call a month following up on the letter you wrote, a promise to organize an advocacy training for your church, or a letter a week to Congress on a justice-related issue. Make it actionable and attainable!

PRAYER

Lord, give me courage to take risks the way Esther did and to challenge injustice, even if it is at great cost to me. Help me to steward my voice and advocate for justice with my elected officials. Be with our president and members of Congress who make major decisions that affect people all over the world. Give them wisdom, tenderness, and sensitivity to the cries of the impoverished.

---

9 Use the fact sheet on pp. 117-119 as a starting point for your research on PFDA

10 Use the fact sheet on pp. 122-124 as a starting point for your research on corruption

JUSTICE AND PRAYER

CHANGING THE WORLD, AND CHANGING OURSELVES THROUGH PRAYER

Prayer is also the integration of coming in our dependence, weakness, finitude, and longing, asking for God's power to do what we need, for our sake and the sake of others.
–Mark Labberton

We are to change the world through prayer. **–Richard J. Foster**

DEFINITIONS

CHARLES TAYLOR

Former leader of a rebel group that fought to overthrow the Liberian government in the 1990s, afterwards becoming president of Liberia. Due to his oppressive regime and alleged war crimes within Sierra Leone and Liberia, he left office in 2003. In April 2012, he was convicted of war crimes and crimes against humanity on charges including terror, murder, and rape.

CUPBEARER

Nehemiah's role for King Artaxerxes. The position of cupbearer was one of the most trusted positions in the court, as the cupbearer was the one who tested and made sure that all of the king's food and drink weren't poisoned before he consumed them. As a result of this role, Nehemiah was in a place of great influence with the king.

INTERCESSORY PRAYER

The act of praying to God on behalf of others.

WE ARE TIRED OF RUNNING

BY ASHLEY WALKER

From 1989 until 2003, the Liberian civil war raged, leaving the country and its people absolutely devastated. Two to three hundred people were massacred daily, gang rape became commonplace, and people were constantly being displaced from their homes. One day, a woman named Leymah Gbowee had a strange dream of God telling her to "gather up the women and pray for peace."

And she did exactly what God called her to. She began with a handful of women in a fish market praying for peace. In a beautiful display of God's love, both Christian and Muslim women gathered in public places and sang and prayed for peace. They took wild, nonviolent actions such as organizing a sex strike, sit-ins, fasts and taking over public places to sing, worship, and pray for peace. Their mantra rang out:

We are tired of war. We are tired of running. We are tired of begging for bulgur wheat. We are tired of our children being raped. We are now taking this stand to secure the future of our children because we believe, as custodians of society, tomorrow our children will ask us, "Mama, what was your role during the crisis?"

After several months, President Charles Taylor granted the women a hearing. They successfully urged him to attend peace talks in Ghana that would take place in June 2003.

Gbowee led the women to the peace talks in Ghana to ensure that progress was made. When she found that the leaders were not taking the process seriously, they sat down in the halls where the talks were taking place, essentially holding everyone in the room hostage until an agreement was definitively made. A settlement was reached, the peace agreement was signed, and in August 2003, the civil war officially ended—just one year after Leymah and the women of the fish market began praying passionately for peace.

PASSIONATE PRAYER FOR JUSTICE

BY KYLE STILLMAN & JASON FILETA

I've noticed that I often see prayer not as an action itself but as a predecessor to my "real" action. I think many of us do. We open meetings with prayer; we pray to kick off big events, but what about prayer as action? Prayers like Nehemiah's, like Leymah's in Liberia, that change the world? Prayer changes us, changes our world, and sustains us in the long and difficult struggle to live justly.

Many of us pray daily for our families and loved ones. We also send sporadic, urgent prayers in times of great need—when the challenges of life seem so overwhelming that we don't know what else to do. In seeking justice, this will always be the temptation. The challenges of hunger, gender equality, slavery, and extreme poverty are all much bigger than we can manage. At best, we fire shotgun prayers; at worst, we fail to pray for massive change. What if we prayed as faithfully as Nehemiah or as Leymah for an end to hunger? For an end to slavery? What if we prayed with the same fervor for our brothers and sisters in extreme poverty as we would for our own children?

I have no doubt that these prayers would not only change us—convict us, give us wisdom for more and better action, sustain us in the overwhelming struggle—but would also change our leaders, those in power, and ultimately the world. As we pray and encounter God, we can't help but be spurred to action. In other words, the more we pray about an issue, the more we realize what we can do. Prayer is empowering!

We read that in the midst of Nehemiah's moment of fear, he quickly prayed to God for wisdom. As the story goes, Nehemiah's words convinced the king to let him leave his servitude and lead a revival whose cornerstone was rebuilding Jerusalem's walls—an act of protection, defiance, and justice.

It would be a mistake to view this as Nehemiah's shotgun prayer. When we read the beginning of the story, we see that Nehemiah spent the days before this encounter with the king fasting, confessing, praying, and humbling himself in the name of his people before God. It was this prolonged intimate time with God that allowed him to have such a bold and successful encounter with Artaxerxes.

There is no doubt that when Nehemiah heard the sad news of his homeland and its dire state, his heart was burdened. In fact, we read that, immediately after he heard about Jerusalem, he sat down, weeping and mourning for days. But his first response was one of humility and honesty—he knew he was powerless to change the circumstances and needed to petition God for his divine intervention.

When it comes to the call to pursue justice, we can react similarly to Nehemiah. We hear news of modern slavery around the world, we see people wandering our streets due in part to systems they can't overcome, we read about families stricken by poverty and unable to send their children to school or even feed them nutritious food, and we feel the need to get involved somehow. We try to figure out which organizations can be trusted and which ones need to be reformed, we realize it's a near impossible task, and can feel overwhelmed at our powerlessness.

Bringing justice to the world isn't going to be accomplished by us, but by God.

Nehemiah models for us how we ought to respond: through passionate prayer and inspired action. After Nehemiah began rebuilding the wall, he encountered great opposition from those directly opposed and even threats of violence. But once again, Nehemiah called the people to God's mission of justice and right living; once again, he sought counsel from God in prayer and God sustained him in his struggle. Nehemiah knew that his work was not his own to accomplish but was God's design for his people— this gave him a sense of resting in God's power, not his own. Bringing justice to the world isn't going to be accomplished by us, but by God.

We imitate his heart in seeking justice for the vulnerable in our neighborhoods and in the world. He lends us his compassion and his dream for restoration. It's his hope to see his creation restored to wholeness, so we pray passionately for justice to be done, "thy kingdom come, thy will be done on earth as it is in heaven"; we pray for God to change us, to make us sensitive to the cries of injustice, and for the wisdom and courage to act; and finally, we pray for God to sustain us in the struggle. The battle is His, so we rest in His power.

NEHEMIAH 1 & 5

QUESTIONS

1. How often do you pray? Are there things you pray for daily?
2. Do you pray about "big" issues like hunger, slavery, and extreme poverty? What do those prayers look like?
3. How does Nehemiah's prayer life empower him to have confidence in pursuing justice for God's people? How can we pray in the same way for our context?
4. Share a time when your prayers were clearly answered.
5. What is God saying to you, and what are you going to do about it?

TOGETHER

Print pictures that represent strength, power, and wealth— pictures of Wall Street, politicians, or corporate logos. Print pictures that represent the most vulnerable people and places in our world—children, widows, a map of an impoverished community with which you are familiar.

As a group, look at these pictures side by side and pray that the vulnerable might influence the powerful and that the powerful will use their strength to seek justice for the vulnerable. Pray specifically for our leaders and the decisions they make that affect the vulnerable in our nation and around the world.

SOLO WORK

Continue working on your action plan by adding a prayer plan. Remember to make your long-term commitment actionable!

On top of your long-term commitment, challenge yourself to pray about an issue that seems too big or too overwhelming, and pray daily for a month. This will train you to come to God persistently and prayerfully in the face of injustice.

Additionally, consider one way in which you will organize your community to be in prayer?

Keep working on your creative expression.

PRAYER

Lord, give me the dedication of Nehemiah to see justice done even in the face of adversity. Draw me close to you, and your heart, and your concerns. Give me sensitive ears, and eyes to hear and see injustice, and courage to respond.

JUSTICE AND CONSUMPTION

EVERY PURCHASE MATTERS

The witness to simplicity is profoundly rooted in the biblical tradition, and most perfectly exemplified in the life of Jesus Christ.
-Richard J. Foster

When we recognize that the people who make our stuff have hopes, dreams, and personalities, we can't help but care about whether their job pays them a living wage and allows them to reach those dreams. **-Kelsey Timmerman**

DEFINITIONS

FAIR TRADE

A structure of selling and purchasing goods that promotes accountability for businesses to compensate workers fairly and justly. Products and businesses that bear a "Fair Trade" emblem are approved by fair trade organizations that monitor trade activity to ensure an environment of justice.

SUPPLY CHAIN

The steps in production within a network of companies to move a product or service from supplier to customer.

SIMPLICITY

An attitude that cultivates a lifestyle of modesty in consumption. When we choose to live simply, we consume less, which in turn aids in the decreased demand for goods produced cheaply and often unjustly.

FAIR TRADE CAN MAKE ALL THE DIFFERENCE

BY ASHLEY WALKER

Today, over a billion people are living in extreme poverty ($1.25 or less per day), with most of this population working in the agricultural sector. Many of the items we enjoy daily come from companies trying to keep up with a competitive market. To do this, they must continually lower their prices. This means that they continually pay the farmers and producers less and less, often cheating them out of funds they deserve.

A low price at the grocery store often means someone was not paid well for his or her work, safety considerations were lowered, the environment was treated harshly, and/or communities of workers were not taken care of. That doesn't sit well with you, does it?

"Fair trade" means that the company involved fairly pays the workers, provides ethical working conditions, has transparency in their operations, and uses earth-friendly practices. Fair trade products ensure that the farmers or workers will receive a guaranteed minimum price that will meet their needs and create stability, though it may exceed this minimum. This allows the farmers to treat their workers, the community, and the earth with equal fairness.

Gerardo Arias Camacho left his farm and family in the 80s because coffee prices were so low that he actually would have fallen into debt if he had tried to produce it. In his town, there was no school for his children or any form of infrastructure (such as paved roads or bridges) at all. He went to the United States to work for the next ten years until he had saved up enough funds to buy the family coffee farm from his parents. Gerardo became Fair Trade certified, and he can count on established prices. His farm also receives a Fair Trade Premium, which gives him additional money that can be invested in the community.

Now Gerardo has a stable farm, a scholarship program for local students, improved roads and other infrastructure within his community, and improvements on his farm. He uses fewer pesticides, his work requires little to no deforestation, and he gains energy through excess waste (e.g., coffee skins). This is a sustainable practice that anyone can join, but there must be demand. Shopping for Fair Trade items creates demand and hope for a more sustainable and ethical world that we can all be a part of.

PURCHASING POWER

BY SHAYNE MOORE
AND KIMBERLY MCOWEN YIM

I don't know about you, but I like to find a good deal. Often, when people compliment me on what I'm wearing, I reply with, "Thanks!" and then go into the backstory of what a great deal it was. Why is it, when I buy something nice that's inexpensive, I think I'm a smart shopper?

Recently, I have been convicted by my "cheap is better" mentality. I will always want a good value, but now I pause at the point of purchase and ask questions. "Why is this so cheap? I wonder if the person who made this was paid a fair wage."

Our global economy has created a marketplace for cheap labor, and although slavery has been documented in nearly all types of consumable goods production, it is still very difficult to identify and therefore eliminate. From cars to clothes to food, every industry uses commodities tainted by slavery.

It is important that companies hear from their customers. Without that input, many will continue to make decisions based only upon their bottom line. We, the consumers, are the last link in the supply chain. Therefore, we have considerable power. "By speaking in one voice, consumers can bring enough pressure to bear to remove the slavery ingredient from the things we buy," writes Kevin Bales, president of Free the Slaves. As consumers, we can begin to ask our favorite companies what they are doing to be part of the solution in building a slave-free economy.

In 2001, reports surfaced about human trafficking and child labor perpetuated by individuals within the chocolate industry. Consumers were outraged to discover that child labor, child trafficking, and other human rights abuses existed on the cocoa farms of the Ivory Coast, a nation that produces over half of the world's chocolate.

Two members of Congress, Senator Tom Harkin of Iowa and Representative Elliot Engel of New York, responded to the cries and proposed an addition to an agriculture bill that would require a federal system to certify and label chocolate products as "slave-free."

What these two legislators did was significant. They started a push to put real pressure on the largest companies that buy cocoa from the small farms accused of child slavery and then manufacture chocolate and make billions of dollars a year in revenue worldwide. The measure passed the House of Representatives, and the leading chocolate manufacturers have been forced to take action to address the issue.

Many people claim that, in our global economy, it's too difficult to address the supply chain and to guarantee slave-free products. However, we believe that nothing is too hard or justifies the enslavement of other human beings. It might be challenging, but it is not impossible.

Companies spend millions of dollars on marketing strategies to get our attention and build a relationship with us to get us to buy their products. They create surveys, campaigns, and advertisements all in hopes that their investment will pay off later in our exchange of money for their services or goods. We need to let them know that we care whether men, women, and children are enslaved to make the products we buy. We need to communicate to our favorite companies and brands that we will put our money toward those that are honestly and transparently working toward a slave-free economy.

The question remains: what can be done? If international labor laws, U.S. legislation, agreed-upon protocols for industry standards, local governments and police have not been willing or able to stop the problem, what are we to do as ordinary consumers?

Where do we go from here? Do we throw our arms up in defeat and refuse to buy or eat chocolate? Do we boycott Hershey's and Nestle?

There is an alternative – fair trade.

Fair trade is defined as *"a system of exchange that honors producers, communities, consumers, and the environment. It is a model for the global economy rooted in people-to-people connections, justice, and sustainability."*

Fair trade chocolate and other products have begun to take a more prominent role on our grocery shelves and in the consumer's conscience. Fair trade labeling can be seen on coffee, chocolate, and many other products. Any product labeled "Fair Trade" must undergo an independent third-party certification process that assesses the poverty, sustainability, and empowerment of the workers in the world's most impoverished countries.

While fair trade isn't seen as a perfect system by anyone, it is a tool that consumers can use to vote with their dollars. It is a way to begin supporting flourishing with our consumption choices rather than perpetuating exploitation.

With power comes responsibility. I have come to believe that, when it comes to my purchasing power, I should begin by praying for wisdom. This is countercultural thinking in a world where impulse buying and the "we want what we want" mentality is embedded in our consumption habits. In slowing down and thoughtfully questioning how things are made and produced, we will be able to reallocate our spending to slave- free items that we need and begin to understand what real value is: when all lives are treated with dignity.

JEREMIAH 22:13-17

QUESTIONS

1. What are the injustices found in this passage?
2. Contrast the wealth of King Josiah and his sons. What does the source of their wealth say about their trust in God?
3. Do you know who the workers are that sustain your life? Share with the group about one way you try to seek justice with your consumption.
4. What is God saying to you, and what are you going to do about it?

TOGETHER

Grab a computer and head over to slaveryfootprint.org. Have one person volunteer to take the test to see how many slaves work for you (no judging; you'll all be taking the test soon enough!).

As a group, reflect on this information and talk about one thing you could do together in response for the remainder of *Live Justly*. Perhaps you make coffee each week—promise to buy only Fair Trade coffee. Perhaps your group eats a meal together—consider embracing intentional simplicity by forgoing the meal every other meeting to put those resources toward a cause.

SOLO WORK

Research one store that you buy goods from often. Find out how this company treats its employees, where it manufactures its goods, and how it spends its revenue.

- Does this influence your desire to continue buying goods from this company? How can you re-assign your consumption to more justice-oriented companies? Come prepared to share your findings with the group.

- Add a "consumption" piece to your action plan. Start by taking the test at slaverfootprint.org. Make your plan specific—maybe you commit to buy only Fair Trade coffee or used clothing—pick one thing you can make actionable and embrace in the long haul!

Continue work on your Creative Expression and find one person to share your thoughts, ideas, and even your project itself with to get feedback and to help you create coherently.

PRAYER

Lord, forgive me for the times I consume goods selfishly or unwisely, without regard for my impact on others. Help me to be aware of how I consume on a daily basis and how I can promote the flourishing of others through my choices. Help me to live justly in the area of consumption, not as a Pharisee seeking to keep the "justice" laws but rather as an act of worship toward you.

JUSTICE AND GENEROSITY

JUSTICE WILL COST YOU SOMETHING

If our giving does not at all pinch or hamper us, I should say it is too small. There ought to be things we should like to do and cannot because our commitment to giving excludes them.
-C.S. Lewis

We have been brainwashed to believe that bigger houses, more prosperous businesses, and more sophisticated gadgets are the way to joy and fulfillment. As a result, we are caught in an absurd, materialistic spiral. The more we make, the more we think we need in order to live decently and respectably. Somehow we have to break this cycle because it makes us sin against our needy brothers and sisters and, therefore, against our Lord. And it also destroys us. Sharing with others is the way to real joy. **-Ron Sider**

DEFINITIONS

SACRIFICIAL GIVING

Intentionally giving something that is precious or costly to you as an act of worship or devotion: giving from our substance rather than abundance. Sacrificial giving is a choice to give up something that might bring you comfort or joy to give to others who are in need.

THE $50,000 QUESTION, LITERALLY

BY JASON FILETA

Nearly eight years ago, I encountered a man that I will never forget. I had just finished speaking about biblical justice at a university chapel, and I invited the students and faculty into meaningful action with Micah Challenge. Afterwards, I was bombarded with encouragement and conversations from people this message touched and resonated with. Eight years later, I don't remember any of their names or faces except one man, whom we'll call Tom.

Tom came to me and told me how God had been speaking to him and his wife on the topic of justice and generosity. They were convinced that the need in the world was so great that their response must match the need. He asked me what he should do with $50,000. I was floored. I had no idea. I told him we should talk further, as five minutes after a chapel talk isn't enough time to dig into the matter.

Later that day over coffee, he told me more about their desire to give sacrificially, and it grew completely out of their understanding that Christ gave himself sacrificially that we might have life. They had decided, in fact, that their potential need in the future (retirement) was not as important as the urgent needs of those today who will die of hunger, malaria, and other preventable causes. Tom came to me with a check in his chest pocket, prepared to write away his retirement fund to meet the urgent needs of the impoverished. This is how ready he was to give all.

He didn't get to this place overnight or because of my 20-minute chapel talk. He arrived here, first, out of a deep understanding of Christ's sacrifice for him, second out of his own understanding and awareness of the needs in the world, and finally by conviction from the Holy Spirit. Tom was ready to give more than I had ever been, and that is why I'll never forget his name, his face, his story, his $50,000, or the sacrifice he was willing to make for the cause of justice.

LIVING A LIFE OF GENEROSITY

BY EUGENE CHO[11]

Generosity does not have to be just a transactional experience. We can experience so much more joy and spiritual impact with our philanthropy.

From time to time, my wife Minhee and I try to step back from our giving, look at the big picture, and then develop a strategy about how and why we give. We experienced a big shift a few years ago in how we saw our finances. When I realized that 80% of the world lives on less than $10 dollars a day, it compelled a shift in how we saw our role in the larger world.

At that time, as a single-income family living in Seattle, we were just trying to get by. It felt laborious at times since Seattle is an expensive city. It's a challenge. We had a mortgage, car payments, bills, and all that stuff. We also have three kids. They like to eat. Like every day. Like five times a day.

Sooner or later, you get into the mindset that you do not have enough. You start comparing yourself with others. I get stressed and insecure when I hear of other parents saving up for their kids' 529s and their IRAs and other

11 From *Overrated* by Eugene Cho. Used by permission of David C. Cook, 4050 Lee Vance View, Colorado Springs, Co. All Rights Reserved.

technical financial terms that I'm still not entirely sure I understand.

One paradigm shift helped me take a step back and see the big picture of my finances: I added up my salary over my 40 years of life. In doing so, I realized that I am a millionaire.

At an annual salary of $68,000, without factoring in salary increases, I've earned about $2.7 million. That's a lot of money. I know there are day-to-day and month-to-month expenses, tithing, taxes, and many other commitments, but it was helpful for me to get a big-picture perspective and thus a grander vision of how I can live generously.

Money influences many of the major decisions in the countries where we live, too, filtering down to our communities, churches, and neighborhoods. I believe that, when we look at the whole picture, **it's rare for major decisions to favor the world's poorest.** This is why we must advocate for the poor. This is why we, as followers of Jesus Christ, must fight for the rights of the poor.

So many of us want to serve Christ, but we want to serve Him on our terms. We want to ask people towards generosity without the personal commitment to live generously. I'm reminded of a man Jesus met, a man we know as the rich young ruler. He was an upstanding, religious man who was trying to serve the Lord. He approached Jesus with a question for which he likely already had answers in mind:

Just then a man came up to Jesus and asked, "Teacher, what good thing must I do to get eternal life?"

"Why do you ask me about what is good?" Jesus replied. "There is only One who is good. If you want to enter eternal life, keep the commandments."

"Which ones?" he inquired.

Jesus replied, "You shall not murder, you shall not commit adultery, you shall not steal, you shall not give false testimony, honor your father and mother, and love your neighbor as yourself."

"All these I have kept," the young man said. "What do I still lack?"

Jesus answered, "If you want to be perfect, go, sell your possessions and give to the poor, and you will have treasure in heaven. Then come, follow me."

When the young man heard this, he went away sad, because he had great wealth.

Matthew 19:16-22

Jesus ministered to the rich young ruler. Jesus pierced this young ruler's soul and knew that greed held him captive. Jesus knew that money was his idol, and this idol prevented him from growing in faith, trust, and discipleship.

Think about the rich young ruler for a moment. Wealth. Youth. Power. Triple gold.

We have to ask ourselves a question here. Is it possible that Christ might be challenging us to live life with loose hands? I don't know about you, but I have a hard time seeing myself as the rich young ruler. I'm not rich, I'm no longer young, and I'm certainly not a ruler. And yet, I have all the comforts that this young man enjoyed and more. Perhaps we are much more like the rich young ruler than we imagine. I can't help but be challenged by these words from E. Stanley Jones, the 20th century Methodist missionary and theologian: "Money is a wonderful servant but a terrible master. If it gets on top and you get under it, you will become its slave."

Philanthropy and generosity are not reserved for the elite. You don't have to be a rock star, a millionaire, or a celebrity to be generous. The root word of "philanthropy" literally means "love of humanity," and this is something we can all do. This is something we must all do. This kind of love can change the world. And when we live this simple truth, we'll be changed ourselves.

ISAIAH 58:4-10

QUESTIONS

1. It is clear in Isaiah 58 that God wants us to "spend" ourselves--this means giving of ourselves. How do you define giving sacrificially?
2. What does the passage describe as the benefits of living generously?
3. Fasting is often considered a form of worship that shows great devotion. What does Isaiah 58 teach of about acts of justice and generosity as worship?
4. What would it look like to reorient our attitude towards worship to include seeking justice?
5. What is God saying to you, and what are you going to do about it?

TOGETHER

Today, you will all leave with one less thing than you came with. Empty your pockets. Yep, right now. Practicing generosity when we least expect it is a good reminder of our posture toward our posessions. Everything we have is God's, as a reminder of that today, offer up the cash in your pocket, the shoes on your feet, or the watch on your wrist. Put these in a pile in the middle of the room and snap a photo. Make sure everyone gets a copy of the photo— keep it as a reminder of sacrificial giving.

Collectively decide where to donate these things, but more significantly, pray that this will be more than an exercise, the beginning of great sacrifice in your lives for justice. The photo will always be a reminder of the radical generosity that God calls us to.

SOLO WORK

Examine your heart. What is holding you back from giving generously and sacrificially? Take a moment to pray and listen. It could be a trust issue, it could be a sense of ownership over your money and time, it could be a selfish desire to have more, etc.

Write down the barriers you have to giving.
How can you sacrificially give of yourself moving forward? Come up with one to three promises, ideas for your action plan related to giving more of yourself—your money, your time, and/or your energy.

Continue to work on your Creative Expression.

PRAYER

Lord, challenge me to be as generous as you are, to give freely of what I have, because everything I have has been given to me by you.

SESSION EIGHT
JUSTICE AND RELATIONSHIPS
AUTHENTIC RELATIONSHIPS ARE THE HEART OF JUSTICE

And that's when things get messy. When people begin moving beyond charity and toward justice and solidarity with the poor and oppressed, as Jesus did, they get in trouble. Once we are actually friends with the folks in struggle, we start to ask why people are poor, which is never as popular as giving to charity.
-Shane Claiborne

DEFINITIONS

JUSTICE PHARISEE

When seeking justice becomes legalistic in the same way the Pharisees were legalistic in upholding the law.

SACRIFICED ON THE ALTAR OF 'JUSTICE'

BY JASON FILETA

Picture the scene: me, a young idealistic organizer for Micah Challenge USA in New York City for the United Nations. I was sitting at the dinner table with men I hoped to emulate. These were my living heroes, men who led internationally known and respected justice organizations, here at the UN to give testimony, speak at rallies, and urge global leaders to keep their promises to the impoverished.

They challenged me to have authentic relationships with the impoverished, to stand with the oppressed rather than for the oppressed. They were some of the few voices in New York that week lifting up the voices of the oppressed—telling their stories and bringing their concerns to halls of power that most people in extreme poverty would never have the chance to speak in.

I had read their books, had paid money to hear them speak on several occasions, and prayed that one day I might become like them ... that is, until we reached dessert.

One leader asked another about his son. His response was something along the lines of, "He's OK, out of treatment now, but still not sure who he is or what he is doing."

One by one, they all shared the deeper struggles of their families. Broken relationships with children, estranged children, drug abuse, alcoholism, suicide attempts, depression, and the list goes on. My heart hurt for them, but I also wondered how men who bring so much healing to the world could have so much brokenness in their own homes.

After the sharing was complete, one of them raised his glass and said, "Well, what we do isn't easy on the family, is it?"

And to that, we clinked our glasses and drank. I decided at that moment that I no longer wanted to be like them, that there had to be a better way—that my calling to seek justice did not have to come at the expense of my calling as a husband or father. If it did, then whose justice was I seeking? *Certainly not God's,* I thought. Little did I know that would take years for me truly to learn this lesson.

So often when we think of relationships and justice, we think of how those in positions of power must be in genuine, dignified, authentic relationships with those in oppression. This is an important conversation, but we must also consider our personal relationships with those God has called us to walk through life with—our families and loved ones.

Don't get me wrong—justice will always cost us something, but the currency of our families and loved ones is far too precious to be sacrificed on the altar of "justice."

RELATIONSHIP: THE FOUNDATION OF JUSTICE

BY SUNIA GIBBS

Where I live and work, I can't walk a block without seeing or passing someone who is homeless. When I first moved into the city, there were mornings I would walk out my front door and find one or two individuals taking shelter on the porch to avoid the rain or sleeping off a hard night. In the beginning I wanted to give and share with every single person. I handed out sleeping pads and blankets, shared food, prayed, and offered advice.

But the longer I lived in the city, the more I gave, and the more frequently I heard a knock on my door, the more I became tired and numb. The need was never ending, but my compassion was not. I felt used. I worried about how much I could give without compromising my children or our home, and I didn't really know whether anything I was doing even mattered. I was disillusioned and disappointed.

To endure in the work of justice, we must determinedly walk through the wastelands produced by greed, lust, and loss and not run when overwhelmed with disparity. The antidote for quitting or disillusionment is not simply greater zeal but increased love and compassion that comes from the Spirit of God living in each of us.

Every relationship, from our immediate family members to a stranger we care for ought to be founded, directed, and empowered by love. In 1 Corinthians 13:3, Paul tells us that, if we give everything to the poor or even become martyrs but do not have love, there is no benefit.

This is an important reminder for those who dedicate their lives to the work of justice. The just life we are called to live cannot ignore the needs of our spouses or children or closest friends. At the same time, the just life we are called to live cannot ignore the needs of our brothers and sisters on the street or around the world because their burden is ours. Jesus demonstrated the solidarity we ought to have in Matthew 25:40 when he said, "Whatever was done to the least of these who are members of my family, you did it to me." These words brought encouragement to the disciples who were being sent into the world. They would remember that whatever was being done to them was felt and known by Jesus, their brother, Savior, and friend. As the body of Christ, are we aware of the pain in other parts of the body? How can we act/speak in solidarity with one another just as Christ does for each of us?

Love for God and love for neighbor empower and eradicate the distance between every human being. When we begin truly to comprehend that the Word became flesh and walked with us (John 1:14), we will have a deeper understanding of humility and self-sacrificing love. Think of it: the One who is Divine and Holy put on frail humanity and made his home with us. Emmanuel—God with us.

Every relationship, from our immediate family members to a stranger we care for ought to be founded, directed, and empowered by love.

Who are we with? If we ignore or avoid the vulnerable around us, how can we be motivated to act with them for deliverance? If our eyes only see people exactly like us, if we just work really hard to purchase shiny new objects, or if all our energy is spent striving for higher positions of power or fame, we have given in to the values of the world around us instead of becoming more and more responsive to the Spirit of God, who reminds us of our abundance and compels us to go deeper and generously into our communities.

Jesus lived with the poor. He saw them and was moved with compassion and met their needs. Are we empowered and free to do the same? 1 John 3:16-18 encourages us in this way: *"We know love by this, that he laid down his life for us—and we ought to lay down our lives for one another. How does God's love abide in anyone who has the world's goods and sees a brother or sister in need and yet refuses help? Little children, let us love, not in word or speech, but in truth and action."*

Who are we with? If we ignore or avoid the vulnerable around us, how can we be motivated to act with them for deliverance?

We demonstrate love through our relationships with one another. And this love must be more than the words we speak but also the actions we take to relieve one another's burdens. It is the only way our love can be sincere. It is the way in which we prove we know God's love—it's not in how many verses we've memorized or in keeping our religious rituals but in how we love one another.

May our relationships with one another radiate and demonstrate the abundant and generous love of God. May we have the courage and empowerment to live justly with and toward one another.

MATTHEW 25:31-46

QUESTIONS

1. Jesus says that what we do to the "least of these" we do to him. What does this say about the nearness of Jesus to the "least of these"? How does this change the way we respond as we encounter the vulnerable?
2. In the passage, the people on the left are said to have refused to help those in need. In our modern world, many of our encounters with those in need aren't face to face. How do we refuse those we know about but don't know personally?
3. What is God saying to you, and what are you going to do about it?

TOGETHER

Humility and vulnerability should be at the core of all of our relationships. In the context of seeking justice, this is true both with the impoverished and with our loved ones. This next exercise is a practice in both!

Have someone in the group read John 13:1-17. During the reading, begin taking off your shoes and socks. Once you are all barefoot, have the person read it again. Let the reality of this incredible act of humility, the Son of God washing the feet of his disciples, sink in.

Start praying together as a group for you to form authentic relationships with one another, for opportunities to be in relationship with people in oppression, and for strong relationships with your loved ones. Pray as the Holy Spirit leads you.

As you are praying, have one person begin by washing the feet of the person on his or her left. Afterwards, that person washes the feet of the next person to the left, and so on until all of you (who wish to) have participated.

SOLO WORK

Reflect on your own relationships. Make a list of the 10 people you engage with most regularly. What does the list tell you?

Are all the people on the list of the same ethnicity as you? Are they all of the same socioeconomic status as you?

The list could indicate that you are very family-oriented, very connected to your church community or your neighborhood. Who is missing from this list that you wish were on it?

Think of three ways you can stretch yourself in relationships this year—perhaps make a commitment to get to know a refugee family in your neighborhood, to befriend an immigrant family from church, or simply to reach out to a family member you've become distant from. Put this into your action plan.

PRAYER

Lord, help me to remember that your heart is for the people, not just for the cause. Give me a tender heart toward those experiencing injustice, and keep me from apathy. As I passionately seek justice, help me not to do so at the expense of my family and friends, and may my pursuit of justice bring my entire community closer to you.

JUSTICE AND CREATION CARE

GOD WANTS ALL CREATION TO FLOURISH!

Many issues in life are confusing. This one is clear. Many concerns can wait until tomorrow. This one won't. Our planet is in crisis. Creation is groaning. Our neighbors are suffering. The time for Christians to take a stand is now. **-Ben Lowe**

It is not possible to love an unseen God while mistreating God's visible creation. **-John Woolman**

DEFINITIONS

CREATION CARE

Active restoration and concern for the environment for both a positive impact on the environment and a positive impact on humanity.

CLIMATE CHANGE

A change in global or regional climate patterns, in particular a change apparent from the mid- to late 20th century onward and attributed largely to the increased levels of atmospheric carbon dioxide produced by the use of fossil fuels.

PEDRO

BY KIMBERLY HUNT[12]

It's easy to understand why Brazilian farmer Pedro Santana Oliveira has struggled to feed his family when you try to get to his small farm.

The trek to his place in the northeastern state of Pernambuco is so sandy that the tires of any vehicle have difficulty getting traction, and that same sand permeates the soil around his home, making farming extremely difficult.

Access to water in this arid area is a problem. There was once a reservoir, but the changing climate and environmental degradation means it has dried up, leaving Pedro and his neighbors facing seven-mile round trips using donkeys to fetch water from the nearest source.

It's little wonder that many locals are giving up working the land in favor of migrating to Brazil's cities, but many encounter further hardship as they discover their agricultural skills are insufficient to find an urban livelihood.

---

12 From Tearfund UK www.tearfund.org

Due to help from a non-profit in his area, Pedro and his neighbors are able to remain on their ancestral grounds as farmers.

Pedro has had help to install a rainwater harvesting tank to capture whatever falls when the heavens do open, and they have also implemented an irrigation system that uses solar panels to power a pump that moves the water around to serve 20 families! Pedro has now started growing crops again for his family's consumption and hopes to be able to sell them in the market soon.

A changing climate and environmental degradation mean millions go hungry, lack access to clean water, and are living in constant uncertainty. As Christians, God has entrusted us with caring for his creation and all those living within it. We can and should take steps to allow creation to flourish.

SHALOM AND CREATION CARE

BY BEN LOWE, JASON FILETA, & LISA GRAHAM MCMINN

When we think of the need for shalom in the world, it is easy to think first and mainly of human concerns such as the conflict in Syria, Southern Sudan's crisis, and the Israeli-Palestinian conflict.

We rarely think of environmental issues such as pollution, animal suffering, deforestation, and a scarcity of water. But Jesus Christ is the Lord of all, and he is bringing peace and reconciliation to all levels of relationships through his blood shed on the cross:

He is the image of the invisible God, the firstborn over all creation. For by him all things were created: things in heaven and on earth, visible and invisible, whether thrones or powers or rulers or authorities; all things were created by him and for him. He is before all things, and in him all things hold together . . . For God was pleased to have all his fullness dwell in him and through him to reconcile to himself all things, whether things on earth or things in heaven, by making peace through his blood, shed on the cross. (Col 1:15-17, 19-20)

We serve a big God who is in the business of reconciling, through Christ, the entire created order unto himself if nothing less. Working for world peace does not mean focusing first on human wars and thinking about "the rest" later. Everything needs reconciliation, and in God's plan, everything gets it together.

To seek justice in creation is pleasing to God, glorifying to Him, and part of His will for Shalom. In God's Kingdom, there will be no unnecessary animal misery, there will be no drought, and there will be no oil spills. God created all and desires all the brokenness in creation to be restored. In fact, God entrusted us with seeing to it that creation is cared for.

African professor and theologian J.O.Y. Mante says attending to creation is the foundation of all disciplines that are serious about life. Mante says **western theology is ecologically bankrupt.** We spend our best theological energy talking about abstract doctrines such as sanctification, or covenants and dispensations, leaving leave little energy for talking about doctrines connected to living life. **The result is that we live a non-ecological existence that is gradually destroying both human and non-human life.** How, Mante asks, is that Christian?

African theology begins by talking about the fundamentals of life that infuse how Christians live—a theology of food, a theology of power. If we are willing to be humble we may learn something of our blind spots by attending to insights that come from Christians outside our own culture. A critical step towards developing in our theology of creation care is learning from our brothers and sisters around the world for whom care of creation isn't a luxury for the privileged or an optional choice. Its necessity grows out of deep theological understanding and a need for survival.

For some of us, our passion to care for creation came out of our passion to see justice done for people suffering. **In the 21st century we can't adequately care for people without giving some good attention to caring for Earth.** For most of human history Earth provided a seemingly endless supply of resources, but in the last 25 years articles in peer-reviewed, reputable, scientific journals have been showing us that we no longer inhabit a planet with unlimited resources and an endless capacity to absorb the by-products of our lives. **Caring for people, it appears, must now include caring about climate change, deforestation, and species extinctions.**

I recall visiting a rural farmer, Stephen, in northern Uganda. His community was on the verge of famine, and when I asked what caused it, he replied without hesitation, "Climate change." They had lost their growing season three years in a row, the first to drought, the second to floods, and the third once again to drought. For them, climate change wasn't a topic of debate or an optional issue to confront only when a family member brings it up at the dinner table. For Stephen and his community, climate change meant starvation. I came away from Stephen having faced a stark and challenging truth: my relationship with the earth is a justice issue.

We all need Earth's resources to survive, but the complexity comes in knowing how brazenly to approach the harvesting of what we need. Descriptions of felling forests, oil spills, strip mining for coal, packing pigs into "feed lots," and stacking laying hens in cages elicit emotions. Perhaps it provokes defensiveness at a litany that sounds too much like Mother Earth rhetoric, an overvaluing of creation when there are other, more profound human problems confronting us. **With a sound doctrine of creation care, these descriptions of environmental tragedy should instead illicit righteous anger and inspire us to change the world in which we live.**

Whatever emotion this conversation about creation elicits, we primarily invite you to celebrate God's good Earth and to live in ways that fosters the well-being of creation, this beautiful place that we call home. Walking gently is a dance of sorts. It includes enjoying the good gifts of this bounteous Earth while taking no more than we need. **In walking gently, we provide for our children—for all children—and for people and creatures yet to be born.**

It is easy for me to feel shame or guilt about how I live, but it doesn't motivate me to change nearly so much as when I feel inspired to change. Maybe you feel the same. The writer of Hebrews tells us to encourage each other toward perseverance and hope. Let's hold tightly to the hope we say we have while bursting with love and good deeds (Heb. 10:23-24). **May love compel us as we grow our passion for the abundant life that God desires for all, a virtue of care that considers the food we eat, and the energy and resources we consume.**

GENESIS 1:1-2:15

QUESTIONS

1. What is the clearest connection you see between justice for people living in extreme poverty and creation care?
2. What is your theology of creation care? Do you have one?
3. What are some of the ways you try to care for God's creation in your daily life?
4. What is God saying to you, and what are you going to do about it?

TOGETHER

Take a moment and write down three justice issues you are most passionate about. There is no "right" answer here. Create a list that could include things like immigration reform, hunger, trafficking, extreme poverty, or climate change. Share your list with each other, and write down the three issues that are mentioned the most. Now, as a group, begin a discussion about how creation care (or lack of creation care) affects those issues.

Let's take trafficking for example:

- Disaster zones are often the perfect environments for traffickers to thrive.

-People displaced because of famine, lack of water, or natural disaster are vulnerable to being trafficked.

Begin learning together how care for creation and care for people are intertwined.

SOLO WORK

Examine the actions you take in a week that may affect the environment. Look at your recycling habits, water usage, driving habits, food consumption, etc. Add a "creation care" piece to your action plan. Come up with three things you can begin to change about your regular habits that will have a positive effect on creation.

Next week, you will present your action plan to your group! Take some time to polish your action plan. Go back to your previous action commitments and examine them. Perhaps since the session on consumption, God has been speaking to you on something specific related to your purchases. Or maybe prayer for certain people in crisis has really been on your heart in the last few weeks, but this wasn't the case when you wrote your prayer plan.

Remember: keep your goals measurable and time bound. Try to have a minimum of one goal for each session, but don't hesitate to take on more! Be prayerful and intentional as you finish your action plan—allow time and space for the Holy Spirit to speak to you.

PRAYER

Lord, forgive me for actions I have taken that harm your creation. Please guide me to be more aware of protecting the world you have made. Help me see how the actions I take affect not only my surroundings but perhaps also those living in extreme poverty elsewhere in the world. Guide my decisions to live in shalom with all of creation.

SESSION TEN
LIVING JUSTLY
HOW NOW SHALL WE LIVE?

Don't just be aware of injustice. Pursue justice. Don't just pursue justice. Live justly. **- Eugene Cho**

Doing Justice is more than just an action a year, it is a lifestyle.
- Jason Fileta

ELEANOR
BY EUGENE CHO[13]

This is a story about a woman named Dr. Eleanor Sutherland, a family physician in Federal Way, Washington. She died in 2012 after living a life of simplicity that allowed her the flexibility in her time and finances to be extraordinarily generous. Her closest cohorts in serving others were her sister Kathleen and her friend Beatrice.

She grew up extremely poor, so Eleanor elected to attend medical school in Germany, as it was more affordable and was more actively enrolling women. A friend of Eleanor's and the trustee of her estate, Paul Birkey, said that Eleanor cared about health care reform before it became a topic in popular culture. Her version of health care reform was simple: she charged a fraction of the going rate and did not turn anyone away because they couldn't pay.

Paul wrote in an obituary:

13 *Overrated* by Eugene Cho. Used by permission of David C. Cook, 4050 Lee Vance View, Colorado Springs, Co. All Rights Reserved.

Nothing was wasted—if a patient needed a wheelchair, walker, or cane, she would round one up, probably a well-used one. She wheedled pharmaceutical reps for samples she could give away. Perhaps most importantly, each and every patient was listened to carefully and treated in the context of their lives, as a whole person. Her sense of humor was not the ordinary kind; it was an insightful, eloquent, smart-alecky kind—always kind and always present...

Eleanor's boundless passion for medicine, as with her boundless passion for everything, was fueled by and undergirded with her passion to serve God and Jesus Christ. In every way, she led life as a mission with Christ's teachings as her template and guide. Her medical practice, her travels abroad, her everyday life, and her supreme self-confidence all were guided by her all-encompassing faith.

Paul says that, if you knew Eleanor, you had probably been chided for not being sufficiently thrifty. She saved wrapping paper, sat in the dark to save candles, and wore used clothing. She wanted to put herself last so that she would be able to give as Christ taught us to give: generously and unconditionally.

Eleanor died at home, as she wanted, in early 2012. She was 85, leaving a small fortune to charities as a result of her lifestyle—and a legacy of compassion to her friends and clients.

LIVE JUSTLY

BY EUGENE CHO[14]

Everyone loves the idea of justice until there is a cost. Ironically, justice is never convenient, and there is always a cost. This is why we often like "doing justice" or following Jesus up to the point at which it provokes an act of sacrifice that would force us to change how we live or change how we think.

God challenged us to live more simply. He challenged us to give up some of the excess in our lives.

The example of Pope Francis has been refreshing. He took a vow of poverty early in his ministry and has never gone back. Since he was elevated to the papacy, the former Jorge Mario Bergoglio has elected to live in the papal guesthouse, not the four-star accommodations where previous popes lived. He wants people to know that he is with them, not above them. He likes the idea of being in community and close to others rather than on his own, living in luxury.

As the leader of the Church, every pope should act like this. His actions are consistent with what we read about in Scripture. It shouldn't be earth shattering or surprising, and yet the new Pope's behavior is entirely countercultural. His story—early on—of washing feet and welcoming dialogue with laypeople shows his heart and, most importantly, reflects the heart of Christ. The pope is living a life of love and justice.

14 *Overrated* by Eugene Cho. Used by permission of David C. Cook, 4050 Lee Vance View, Colorado Springs, Co. All Rights Reserved.

Jesus loves justice. And justice, by its very nature, involves people. I've learned that people often struggle with Jesus' commitment to justice because he rarely, if ever, spelled out the importance of justice in a three-point sermon. Instead, Jesus lived justly.
Justice was in Jesus.

He reflected justice in how he lived, how he loved, and how he welcomed the stranger, the marginalized, the leper, the widow, the prostitute, and the sick. Jesus reflected justice in how he approached the powers and systems of his age, how he confronted religious leaders, how he embraced, welcomed, and empowered women, and how he confronted ethnic biases and prejudices.

Yes, Jesus loved justice, but even more, he lived justly. And here's the kicker: He called us to follow him.

Justice is not just a thing that is good. Justice is not merely doing good. Justice is not something that's moral or right or fair. Justice is not, in itself, a set of ethics. Justice is not just an aggregation of the many justice-themed verses throughout the Scriptures. Justice is not trendy, glamorous, cool, or sexy. Justice isn't a movement. Justice is so much more, and the understanding of this fullness is central to the work that we do in pursuing justice.

God invites and commands his people not just to be aware of injustice but also to pursue justice. Not just to pursue justice but to live justly. These two acts are not the same, but they are inseparable. To be a follower of Jesus requires us both to pursue justice and to live justly at the same time. This is a truth that ought to inform both our theology of justice and our praxis of justice, and we seek to live this way because, ultimately, justice reflects the character of God. Justice must

Jesus lived justly. Justice was in Jesus.

also then be reflected in the character of his followers.

In seeking to do justice, we must be open to the reality that God will challenge us, change us, and transform us. In doing justice and in doing things that matter to God, we actually grow more in his likeness. We will begin to reflect more of the character of God. We grow more intimate with the heart of God.

We will do things because they embody the Kingdom of God. And it is right in the eyes of God. But in doing these things, there is something equally beautiful in that we become more in tune with the heart of God.

Often, we embody our concept of justice or compassion or generosity when it is about us and our power and privilege to do something for others, without entertaining the possibility that maybe God wants to change us.

We have much to learn from the poor, the marginalized, and the oppressed. We have much to learn from our neighbors who do not look like us, think like us, or act like us. We may even have much to learn from our enemies. There is a level of humility that justice exacts inside us.

The inescapable truth about justice is that there is something wrong in the world that needs to be set right. Sometimes, the things that need to be set right are not just in the lives of those we seek to serve. The things that need to be set right may also be in our own lives.

We need to pursue justice not just because the world is broken but because we're broken, too. Pursuing justice and living a just life every day helps us put our own lives in order. Perhaps this is what God intended—that, in doing his work serving others, we discover more of his character and are changed ourselves.

READING

This session, your final session, together you'll be reading your own words. Continue to the "together" exercise.

TOGETHER

Present your action plans to each other. Offer feedback and come up with ways to hold each other accountable (e.g., accountability partners, emailing each other for specific reminders, setting aside time once a month to check on each other's progress, etc.).

Spend some serious time in prayer together over your action plans.

Complete the Church Justice Evaluation[15] together. Brainstorm three to five things that your small group could do or plan to spur your church toward living justly!

Share your Creative Expressions with one another if you feel so led!

15 The Church Justice Evaluation can be found online at www.livejust.ly

SOLO WORK

Edit your plans based upon the feedback you received from your group. Log on to LiveJust.ly and load your plan to the site. Here, you'll be able to set reminders via email or text, and we'll be able to track the ways in which Live Justly is affecting readers! Finalize your Creative Expression and share it if you feel so led! Use #LiveJustly so we can build a gallery of your creative expressions!

PRAYER

Lord, forgive me for the times I forsake your mission in the world for my own comfort. Guide me as I put this plan of daily justice into action. Help it not to be a checklist I seek to complete each day but let it come from a posture of worship. Give me the endurance, desire, and will to allow justice truly to encompass my actions. Help me to be a person who lives justly. Help me to be more like Jesus.

HELPFUL READING & TOOLS

MICAH DECLARATION ON INTEGRAL MISSION

The Micah Network is a co-founder of Micah Challenge, the publisher of Live Justly. The Micah Network is a coalition of evangelical churches and agencies from around the world committed to integral mission. In 2001, 140 Christians from 50 different countries gathered in Oxford to discuss integral mission and their work in impoverished communities.

Some of the language is dated or not up to our current communication standards, but we left it as is because it is a historical document from a time and place. It is inspiring and inspired! ***This declaration has been foundational to all we do at Micah Challenge. Enjoy!***

INTEGRAL MISSION

Integral mission or holistic transformation is the proclamation and demonstration of the Gospel. It is not simply that evangelism and social involvement are to be done alongside each other. Rather, in integral mission, our proclamation has social consequences as we call people to love and repentance in all areas of life. And our social involvement has evangelistic consequences as we bear witness to the transforming grace of Jesus Christ.

If we ignore the world, we betray the word of God, which sends us out to serve the world. If we ignore the word of God, we have nothing to bring to the world. Justice and justification by faith, worship and political action, the spiritual and the material, and personal change and structural change belong together. As in the life of Jesus, being, doing, and saying are at the heart of our integral task.

We call one another back to the centrality of Jesus Christ. His life of sacrificial service is the pattern for Christian discipleship. In his life and through his death, Jesus modeled identification with the poor and inclusion of the other. On the cross, God shows us how seriously he takes justice, reconciling both rich and poor to himself as he meets the demands of his justice. We serve by the power of the risen Lord through the Spirit as we journey with the poor, finding our hope in the subjection of all things under Christ and the final defeat of evil. We confess that, all too often, we have failed to live a life worthy of this gospel.

The grace of God is the heartbeat of integral mission. As recipients of undeserved love, we are to show grace, generosity, and inclusiveness. Grace redefines justice as not merely honoring a contract but as helping the disadvantaged.

INTEGRAL MISSION WITH THE POOR AND MARGINALIZED

The poor, like everyone else, bear the image of the Creator. They have knowledge, abilities, and resources. Treating the poor with respect means enabling the poor to be the architects of change in their communities rather than imposing solutions upon them. Working with the poor involves building relationships that lead to mutual change.

We welcome welfare activities as important in serving with the poor. Welfare activities, however, must be extended to include movement toward value transformation, the empowerment of communities, and cooperation in wider issues of justice. Because of its presence among the poor, the Church is in a unique position to restore their God-given dignity by enabling them to produce their own resources and to create solidarity networks.

We object to any use of the word "development" that implies that some countries are civilized and developed while others are uncivilized and underdeveloped. This imposes a narrow and linear economic model of development and fails to recognize the need for transformation in so-called "developed" countries. While we recognize the value of planning, organization, evaluation, and other such tools, we believe that they must be subservient to the process of building relationships, changing values, and empowering the poor.

Work with the poor involves setbacks, opposition, and suffering. But we have also been inspired and encouraged by stories of change. In the midst of hopelessness, we have hope.

INTEGRAL MISSION
AND THE CHURCH

God by his grace has given local churches the task of integral mission. The future of integral mission is in planting and enabling local churches to transform the communities of which they are a part. Churches, as caring and inclusive communities, are at the heart of what it means to do integral mission. People are often attracted to the Christian community before they are attracted to the Christian message.

Our experience of walking with poor communities challenges our concept of what it means to be a church. The Church is not merely an institution or organization but a community of Jesus that embodies the values of the Kingdom. The involvement of the poor in the life of the church is forcing us to find new ways of being a church within the context of our cultures instead of being mere reflections of the values of one dominant culture or sub-culture. Our message has credibility to the extent that we adopt an incarnational approach. We confess that, too often, the Church has pursued wealth, success, status, and influence. But the kingdom of God has been given to the community that Jesus Christ called his little flock.

We do not want our church traditions to hinder working together for the sake of the Kingdom. We need one another. The Church can best address poverty by working with the poor and other stakeholders, such as civil society, government, and the private sector, with mutual respect and a recognition of the distinctive role of each partner.

We offer the Micah Network as one opportunity for collaboration for the sake of the poor and the Gospel.

INTEGRAL MISSION
AND ADVOCACY

We confess that, in a world of conflict and ethnic tension, we have often failed to build bridges. We are called to work for reconciliation between ethnically divided communities, between rich and poor, between the oppressors and the oppressed.

We acknowledge the command to speak up for those who cannot speak for themselves, for the rights of all who are destitute in a world that has given "money rights" greater priority than human rights. We recognize the need for advocacy both to address structural injustice and to rescue needy neighbors.

Globalization is often in reality the dominance of cultures that have the power to project their goods, technologies, and images far beyond their borders. In the face of this, the Church in its rich diversity has a unique role as a truly global community. We exhort Christians to network and cooperate to face together the challenges of globalization. The Church needs a unified global voice to respond to the damage caused by it to both human beings and the environment. Our hope for the Micah Network is that it will foster a movement of resistance to a global system of exploitation.

We affirm that the struggle against injustice is spiritual. We commit ourselves to prayer, advocating on behalf of the poor not only before the rulers of this world but also before the Judge of all nations.

INTEGRAL MISSION AND LIFESTYLE

Integral mission is the concern of every Christian. We want to see the poor through the eyes of Jesus, who, as he looked on the crowds, had compassion for them because they were harassed and helpless, like sheep without a shepherd.

There is a need for integral discipleship involving the responsible and sustainable use of the resources of God's creation and the transformation of the moral, intellectual, economic, cultural, and political dimensions of our lives. For many of us, this includes recovering a biblical sense of stewardship. The concept of the Sabbath reminds us that there should be limits to our consumption.

Wealthy Christians—both in the West and in the Two-Thirds World—must use their wealth in the service of others. We are committed to the liberation of the rich from slavery to money and power. The hope of treasure in heaven releases us from the tyranny of mammon.

Our prayer is that, in our day and in our different contexts, we may be able to do what the Lord requires of us: to act justly, to love mercy, and to walk humbly with our God.

27 September 2001

THE ROLE OF GOVERNMENT IN PROMOTING THE FLOURISHING OF COMMUNITIES

A LOOK AT POVERTY FOCUSED DEVELOPMENT ASSISTANCE

Often when we think of prophetic political advocacy, we picture times when brave men and women of faith have stood up to injustice—William Wilberforce ending the transatlantic slave trade, Dr. King fighting against segregation, and the Jubilee movement to cancel odious debts. **Sometimes, however, our role as prophetic advocates is to push our leaders to maintain and expand just policies that cultivate flourishing communities!**

Poverty-focused development assistance (PFDA) is a catchall term describing any foreign assistance given by the U.S. government for the express purpose of poverty alleviation. This helps distinguish it from foreign assistance used for political or military purposes. **The effect of PFDA is astounding and something that we as citizens should be proud of and fight to protect!**

For less than 1% of the federal budget, PFDA is transforming lives and communities around the world!

THE FACTS
Because of poverty-focused development assistance:[16]
- 6.7 million people living with HIV/AIDS receive life-saving anti-retroviral medication.

- More than 22 million children are enrolled in USAID-funded schools.

- Three million children's lives are saved every year through USAID immunization programs.

- 8.8 million children under the age of five have been reached by nutrition programs.

16 All statistics from USAID, UN and World Bank Reports

Another aspect of PFDA we applaud is the role of trusted Christian organizations in implementing assistance.
Organizations such as World Vision, Food for the Hungry, World Relief, and many others have received over $1,000,000,000 (yep, that's $1 billion!) in the last five years alone to do the incredible lifesaving work of providing vaccines, delivering food, providing bed nets to protect against malaria, providing agricultural training, etc.

Here's the thing—this funding is always at risk of being dramatically decreased. Our leaders won't continue to fund programs like these if they don't know where we (the voters) stand. It's time to speak out and encourage our leaders to keep PFDA well-funded!

For more resources to help your group take action, visit www.micahchallengeusa.org. There you will find instructions and resources to help your group

- Call Congress.

- Set up a meeting with your member of Congress.

- Receive a phone briefing from Micah Challenge staff.

- Obtain materials to help you organize a day of action at your church!

We will walk with you as you journey into prophetic advocacy!

CALL SCRIPT
FOR
SESSION FOUR

STEPS TO CALLING CONGRESS WITH YOUR GROUP:

1. Log onto house.gov and type in your ZIP code to see who represents you in the House of Representatives.

2. Call the capitol switchboard at 202-224-3121. They are there 24 hours a day and will forward your call to your member's office.

3. Leave a message either with the staffer who answers the phone or on the machine:

SAMPLE MESSAGE

"Hi, this is <<Your Name>>, a constituent from <<Your City>>. I'm doing a small group study with my church, <<Your Church name>>, on justice. We've just finished learning about the incredible ways foreign assistance has helped people living in extreme poverty. We want to urge Representative <<Your Member's Name>> to be a champion of poverty-focused development assistance. For less than 1% of the federal budget, lives are being saved and communities transformed. ***If leaving a message*** We'd love to hear back from you regarding this important issue. Please call me back at <<Your Number>>. Thank you for your time and your service. We are praying for you."

SOME TIPS FOR YOUR PHONE CALL

- Feel free to make it personal: talk about why you care about people living in extreme poverty.

- You will be educating them—they probably know less about poverty-focused development assistance than you do!

- You are calling on a general issue that will always be relevant, not on a specific bill. Budget negotiations are ongoing, and it never hurts to let a member of Congress know where you stand—with people in extreme poverty!

- Don't be afraid of your faith! If you are in a conversation, feel free to let them know that your faith compels you to stand with the impoverished!

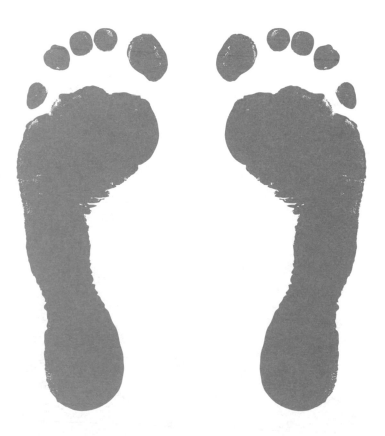

THE ROLE OF GOVERNMENT IN ROLLING BACK INJUSTICE

A LOOK AT CORRUPTION

We have a saying around Micah Challenge: "What happens in the White House affects everyone's house." The reach of our government is immense. The decisions they make have the potential to affect millions of people. In our legislative process, though, impoverished farmers in Mali, school children in India, and migrant workers in Washington have no say in our government's decisions—so who will stand up for them? This is where we come in—as prophetic advocates lifting the concerns of those whose voices are too far away to be heard in the halls of power. **Corruption is one of those concerns that our brothers and sisters around the world have urged us to lift up!**

Corruption is perhaps the biggest barrier to overcoming extreme poverty. We've discovered that the role that U.S. corporations (and U.S. policy regulating those corporations) play in creating the space for corruption to thrive is immense. When money is stolen, when taxes are not paid, and when natural resources are taken in secret, it is the poor who suffer. Money that should be spent on healthcare, education, and development is instead taken by a few. Unfortunately, U.S. corporations, specifically those working in mineral extraction, have been contributing to corruption in impoverished nations for too long.

In response to this, Micah Challenge is shining a light on corruption! Below are some facts and a sample letter you can personalize and send to your representative. Stopping injustice through good policy is something we have the power to influence. Let us shine a light in the darkness!

SHINE A LIGHT: EXPOSE CORRUPTION

The Facts

* The cost of corruption in Africa alone is $148 billion/year [17]

* In India people have paid more than $200 million in bribes[18] annually to access 11 "free" services including police, hospitals, schools, and employment benefits

* Findings from a seven-country study in Africa—Ghana, Madagascar, Morocco, Niger, Senegal, Sierra Leone and Uganda showed that 44 percent of the parents surveyed had paid illegal fees for schools that were legally free for their children.

* Illicit financial flows, including corruption, bribery, theft, and tax evasion, cost developing countries $1.26 trillion per year.[19] This amount of money could lift the 1.4 billion people living on less than $1.25 a day above this threshold for at least six years.

For more resources to help your group take action visit **www.micahchallengeusa.org**. There you will find instructions and resources to help your group:
* Call Congress.

* Set up a meeting with your member of congress.

* Receive a phone briefing from Micah Challenge staff.

* Order materials to help you organize a day of action at your church!

We will walk with you as you journey into prophetic advocacy!

---

17 worldbank.org
18 transparency.org.uk
19 worldbank.org